Xenophobe's Guide to The Israelis

Aviv Ben Zeev

Oval Books

Published by Oval Books
335 Kennington Road
London SE11 4QE
United Kingdom

Telephone: +44 (0)20 7582 7123
Fax: +44 (0)20 7582 1022
E-mail: info@ovalbooks.com
Web site: www.xenophobes.com

Published by Oval Books, 2001

Editor – Catriona Tulloch Scott
Series Editor – Anne Tauté

Cover designer – Jim Wire, Quantum
Printer – Cox & Wyman Ltd
Producer – Oval Projects Ltd

ISBN: 1-902825-34-9

Contents

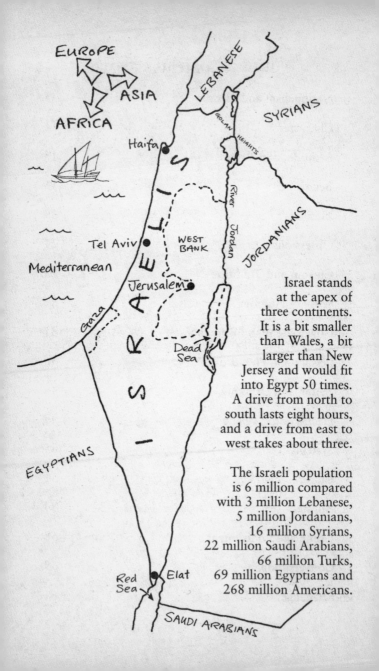

EUROPE

ASIA

AFRICA

LEBANESE

SYRIANS

GOLAN HEIGHTS

Haifa

River Jordan

JORDANIANS

Tel Aviv

WEST BANK

Mediterranean

Jerusalem

Gaza

ISRAELIS

Dead Sea

EGYPTIANS

Red Sea

Elat

SAUDI ARABIANS

Israel stands at the apex of three continents. It is a bit smaller than Wales, a bit larger than New Jersey and would fit into Egypt 50 times. A drive from north to south lasts eight hours, and a drive from east to west takes about three.

The Israeli population is 6 million compared with 3 million Lebanese, 5 million Jordanians, 16 million Syrians, 22 million Saudi Arabians, 66 million Turks, 69 million Egyptians and 268 million Americans.

Nationalism and Identity

Forewarned

"We are on the Map!" declared Tal Brody, the Captain of the Israeli Basketball Team when they won the European Cup Championship. The longing for a place on the map is Israeli nationalism in a nutshell.

In some of its lighter manifestations this may take on a curious face: an Israeli actress landing a role in a Hollywood movie (as the hairdresser who gets shot dead in the opening scene while eloquently uttering her one line: "Ahhh!") is hailed back home as the Keeper of Israel's Place on the Map. The same goes for Israeli soccer players, musicians, Eurovision song contest contenders, writers, public speakers, retired Mosad agents employed overseas as anti-terrorism trainers, models (super and wannabes) – all carry with them, whether they like it or not, the blue and white flag. They are Israelis and are held dear by the silent others watching them and praying: "Please put on a good show! Put us on the Map!"

In many ways Israelis have succeeded in pushing upwards and breaking the surface of international anonymity. For such a tiny state, they occupy mountains of news time (even though the news has not changed in the last 2,000 years, i.e. war, peace and the occasional miracle). Furthermore, since most Biblical scenes occurred in what is now modern Israel, every church sermon everywhere has something to do with Israel and most of the world has at least heard of the holy places.

But many people still believe Israelis ride camels to work and sleep in tents out in the desert (which they do, sometimes, but only on vacation), a belief strongly sponsored by travel agencies. When confronted with flagrant misinformation about their country Israelis tend to be bemused, amused or hurt. But if a foreigner proves knowledgeable about them, they are in his debt for all eternity. He has passed the greatest test of all. He knows who they are and where they are – on the Map.

How They See Themselves

Israelis try not to see themselves too often – literally. When travelling abroad, avoiding their own kind is considered a national sport. An Israeli has the ability to spot a fellow countryman in a crowd of spectators watching a film shoot on a Los Angeles street. He sees him and immediately dislikes him, and if the other notices his glare (as he inevitably will), the feeling becomes mutual. Yet under different circumstances, such as when their backs are to the wall, Israelis stand united like no other nation. Sometimes they secretly long to have their backs to the wall just to be able to feel united.

The reason for this conflict in the Israeli nature is that though united by fate, history and downright patriotism, Israelis see their own faults only too clearly. In the Holy Land everyone is a critic. Israelis know exactly what is wrong with the rest of them (but not necessarily with their individual selves), and are not afraid to voice their criticism – which is, as any psychologist will agree, the first step towards recovery. They know they lack good manners, they resent anyone slightly more successful than they are, they spend hours trying to trick the system, they spend days trying to trick one another and they haggle with everyone about everything.

On the other hand, they take pride in having almost no homelessness in their cities, and as proof of their feelings for their fellows will point to spontaneous public response when money is being raised, for instance, to save a sickly child. An Israeli proverb states 'All Israel are brothers', which is very obvious when landing at Ben Gurion airport. For years this airport has had to handle huge crowds of Israelis awaiting the return of friends and relatives. For every single Israeli returning (even from one week's trip) there are at least five people waiting, teary-eyed. Eventually it became necessary to erect a special Welcoming Hall to contain the throng.

'All Israel are brothers' accounts for the fact that in Israeli apartment buildings all the neighbours know everything about everybody else: their vocation, hobbies, family life, problems and even salary. But if Israelis are likened to brothers, then like brothers they may occasionally engage in fierce quarrels. The fact that the very name Israel means 'to quarrel with God' gives one cause to reflect upon this apparently inherent nature of Israelis, as illustrated by the following joke:

A group of American tourists in Africa was caught by cannibals. The cannibals wanted to eat the prisoners immediately, as custom and hunger dictated, but the tribal chief ordered them to be held in captivity for three months. "Feed the Americans well. Once they're plump, we shall have our feast," he ruled. A week later the same thing occurred to a group of British tourists who were also kept for three months awaiting their fate. When a group of Israeli tourists was captured, the cannibals were about to imprison them for the required three months. This time the chief objected: "These ones are called Israelis and must be eaten at once," he declared, "for if we leave them alone, they will soon eat each other."

The Diaspora

When the Romans, back in A.D. 70, had had enough of constant Jewish revolts in what was then known as the Roman province of Judaea, they burned down the Temple in Jerusalem and sent most of the Jews into exile. Seventy years later another revolt brought an end to the last remnants of Jewish settlement in Judaea: the Romans exiled those involved, and changed the name of the country to Palestine (borrowing it from a small stretch of southern coast). Thus began a period of exile referred to as the Diaspora of the Jews. It lasted some 2,000 years (give or take a few minutes), and during this time Jewish thinking, behaviour, language and culture evolved.

In 1948, when Israel was founded, and the name Palestine receded into the shadows (only to reappear years later), it seemed like a dream to the Jews. Yet at the very moment the vision of a Jewish state became a reality, a split emerged in Jewish identity. The Diaspora Jew was suddenly seen as weak, small and at the mercy of others, while the Israeli Jew was regarded as young, pioneering, free of masters and prepared to fight for his or her country. The contradiction between the Diaspora Jew and the Israeli Jew, the split in identity inside all Israelis, is the root of Israeli character and nationalism.

When Israelis mention Israel amongst themselves, they never say 'Israel', but always '*Ha'Aretz*', meaning literally The Country (with a capital 'T'). When someone is emigrating to Israel he is, in the Hebrew language, 'ascending', and when a person has left Israel for good, he has 'descended', which means he has joined the Diaspora.

Nowadays the Diaspora to many Israelis is where Jews can make lots of money and live an easy life: "What's a Zionist in the Diaspora?" "A Jew who solicits another Jew to give money so that a third Jew can go to Israel." While Israel to Diaspora Jews is a fine concept that bears little financial appeal: "How can you make a million dollars in Israel?" "Start with two."

How They Would Like Others to See Them

Israelis have never accepted themselves as part of the Middle East. It is well known in Israel that when God asked Moses where he would like to lead the Israelites, Moses (who had a severe stutter) had his heart set on

Canada and answered: "Ca...Caan...Caaaan..." "Canaan it is, then," ruled the Almighty. The rest is history.

This is the best explanation Israelis have for the fact that the so-called Chosen Land in reality is one third barren, and has no oil reserves and no friendly mow-the-lawn types as neighbours. They would have liked to be Americans, and would have settled for being Europeans. Israelis therefore would like to be seen as Americanized European pioneers, setting out from lush vegetation and snow-clad mountains to build a modern democratic state in the wilderness.

How They Think Others See Them

Israel is like that girl in school who really cares what everybody is thinking about her, but pretends not to. (She also has a problem with clothes and body odour.)

"The whole world is against us," say Israelis, sometimes jokingly but often seriously, when they are criticised by foreigners. They see the world as divided into roughly three groups: the group that likes them, the group that is vehemently against them, and the group that is totally indifferent to their existence. The last obviously suffers from lack of information and must be educated in order to become part of the first group.

The second group poses a great threat, for it has clearly bonded with the enemy. It is here that some notions get mixed up: if an Israeli gymnast back-flips her way from the bar straight into the lens of the camera at a World Championship, yet receives less than a 9.9, the judges are instantly deemed anti-Semitic. Coming second (or worse) in any kind of international contest is instantly attributed to Middle-East politics in the mind of the enraged Israeli. Fail to welcome a minor Israeli politician to your country and you will be forever labelled 'pro-Arab'. The prevailing principle is: 'You are either with us or against us.'

Those who like Israelis, however, are treated with the kind of warmth, friendship and hospitality reserved for members of the family.

How They See Other Nations

Only a few years ago a trip abroad was something Israelis planned for three months, did for three weeks and then talked about for three years. Nowadays they travel whenever they can. Critic that the Israeli is, whether or not he has come face to face with other nationalities, he has views about the lot. For instance, French people are full of themselves, English youths are violent football fans, Thai people eat dogs, Americans are naïve, Swiss people live in picture postcard surroundings and have everything save a sense of humour, Chinese people emit wise sayings when they are old and Swedish women are attracted to dark-skinned men (Israelis, naturally).

How They See Other Israelis

Israel is a classic immigrant country, which means that in the fifty-odd years of its existence it has had many influxes of immigrants from the four corners of the earth and no opportunity to develop a strong sense of 'us' and 'them'. It's more like 'me' and 'the rest'.

Immigrants land at Ben Gurion airport on a daily basis, sometimes in trickles, at other times in waves of thousands (the 1990s saw more than 600,000 from Russia alone). The problems of assimilation are enormous: the IBA (Israeli Broadcasting Authority) broadcasts in 17 languages. The government runs specialised language schools (Ulpanim) where immigrants study Hebrew as well as get a few pointers about starting life in Israel and the complexities of dealing with the native population.

Israelis will attempt to refrain from voicing biting remarks about newly arrived immigrants, yet as time passes every ethnic group becomes the object of countless jokes. For example, all Israelis know that Persians are considered cheapskates, hence: "Who dug the Suez Canal?" "Some Persian who lost a shekel in the sand." When remarks of this kind are made, it is understood that Jewish immigrants are being portrayed. Israelis will joke about Romanian Israelis being thieves or about Moroccan Israelis slashing others dexterously with switchblades. It's a traditional belief that Polish Israeli women are frigid, Georgian Israeli wives have thicker beards than their husbands, and Iraqi Israelis appear in local films wearing pyjamas in the daytime.

Every Israeli feels free to invent jokes about Israelis of other ethnic origins. It's a national pastime, and nobody takes offence. If you did, you'd be in for a hard time in Israel.

Special Relations

Israelis know who their friends are (though sometimes it is not very evident). They like Americans because America is Israel's big, all-seeing, all-caring uncle (who just happens to have the largest, wealthiest, most active population of Jewish people on the planet). Everybody wants to visit America, to live for a while in America, to have a rich uncle in America, in fact, to be an American.

The fact that America donates billions of dollars-worth of aid to the tiny state of Israel demonstrates the bond between the two nations. Israelis tell of the time the Israeli Minister of Agriculture walked into the office of Prime Minister Levy Eshkol and announced that there was a severe drought looming. The Prime Minister was instantly alarmed: "A drought? This year? That's terrible! Where?" "Why, here in Israel of course," answered the minister. "Ah," sighed Eshkol in genuine relief, "For a second there I thought you meant America."

Israelis tend to have a different relationship altogether when it comes to their immediate neighbours. The issue of the Arabs is so complex that even Israelis have trouble understanding it. The fact that a large percentage of Israelis are themselves Arabs only adds to the confusion. Politics, war and history are thrown into the pot and the rest, most of the time, is CNN material. These days political correctness has moved in, and even the good old jokes about Arabs which used to be regarded as some of the best are only whispered in closed circles and sometimes frowned upon. The world will know peace has truly prevailed in the Middle East only when these jokes once again see the light of day.

Character

According to the Israeli poet Tchernichovsky, 'A man is moulded by the scenery of his native soil'. Imagine yourself living in a hot and dusty climate where the average temperature can make you feel you are about to melt and everything gets on your over-heated nerves. Imagine being submitted to continuous stress from the threat of war so that the ultra-sonic boom of a low-flying jet will send you rushing to the phone to enquire if the attack has begun. Imagine being in a country so small that there is no escape from being recognized on any street of any city by some distant friend of a friend's relative, so you can never do anything you shouldn't.

If you had to endure all this, wouldn't you do almost anything for your Survival? Wouldn't you be the eternal Complainer merely because you are a Worrier? And wouldn't worrying about yourself and about your fellow man inevitably turn you into a Meddler? It can't be helped. Tchernichovsky was right.

Survivalists

Israelis know they are the everlasting survivalists, and it is this trait that underlies some of their characteristics. Over centuries they have learned to extemporise in any situation and to take what they can when it's offered. It is what accounts for their *chutzpa* – audacity.

Where Americans will despatch a team of five people to complete an engineering project, Israelis will send one man who has experience in some aspects of the task and has only heard about the remaining ones. He is the ultimate Israeli, a *kolboynik* (jack of all trades). His product might not be perfect but it will work, and at a third of the cost and time taken by others. Don't bother him with facts, details and plans. Why plan if you can improvise? The basic notion of a start-up company – brains, improvisation and no funds – fits the Israeli ideal of conditions that bring forth results. Multi-million dollar acquisitions of Israeli start-up companies by giants such as Lucent or AOL are evidence that this attitude works.

When opportunity presents itself, Israelis need no second bidding, as illustrated by a group who set out to tour the Scandinavian Alps. Told there would be few stops for food in that day's schedule, they made haste for the breakfast buffet, packed everything in sight and asked for more when the 'supply' ran out. Other guests were appalled, but for the Israelis this was survivalism in practice. As every general knows, troops cannot march on an empty stomach.

It is survivalism that accounts for the Israelis' lack of manners and apparent shamelessness. People who have had to struggle for survival cannot afford the luxury of shame. This attitude is encapsulated by a comedy sketch which portrays an Israeli athlete in the Olympic 100-metre race unashamedly trying to convince the official with the gun to give him a head start: "Haven't we people suffered enough already?" he says, "Do we not have feelings? Be a sport and give me a warning before you fire that thing!"

Complainers

In Israel everybody complains. All the time. About every conceivable thing, be it the weather, the political situation, people's attitudes (excluding one's own of course). 'I complain therefore I am' is the people's maxim. A good complainer (called a *kooter* – derived from the Yiddish for cat), holds the secret of forever being right. Add a headache or a slight illness – giving the complaint a more personal edge – and it just gets better. There's something very emotionally satisfying in complaining, and there's nothing better than doing it in a group, perched on a veranda on a warm Sabbath day, eating watermelon and Bulgarian cheese.

The high point of this general dissatisfaction is reached when the Israeli complains about Israelis complaining too much, without noticing the subtle contradiction.

Worriers

Israelis worry. A common phrase is "*Nu? Az ma yihieh?*" ("So? What's going to happen?"). An Israeli may worry simultaneously about the political situation, security issues, sport, career, family, finance, and dealing with the cockroaches. With all this worrying, people's sense of priorities can become a bit warped. A common Israeli family dialogue could very well be:

"So? What's going to happen with the taxi-drivers' strike?"

"I don't know. It keeps me awake at nights, thinking about it."

"And what about our daughter's imminent divorce?"

"Yeah, that worries me too."

Israelis are aware, of course, that there is little need for all their worrying, but they do like the sensation they experience when they start out expecting the worst and end up being pleasantly surprised.

Meddlers

Israelis cannot resist trying to help their fellow man. This often takes the form of meddling, and can even be mistaken for rudeness. They will interfere in someone else's conversation on the street to offer some good-hearted advice; they will read the newspaper in the hands of the man sitting next to them on the bus and proceed to ask him not to turn the pages so fast; they will never allow a fellow Israeli to fix his car by himself, even against protest.

They simply do not have the same concept of 'minding one's own business' as other nations have. Even in their biggest cities, Israelis will never walk by with their eyes averted should someone trip and fall in the street. They will stop and get involved. In Israel, everything and everybody is everyone else's business. If Israelis keep their bedroom windows closed while being intimate, it is for fear of being shouted at with neighbourly advice.

Attitudes and Values

It's Dire to Be a *Freier*

Israelis grow up with the expression 'never be a *freier*'. A *freier* is a push-over or loser, someone who can be taken for a ride. An Israeli will emerge from a shop after two hours of harsh haggling, which featured name-calling and almost coming to blows with the shopkeeper, with the merchandise in hand and feeling pleased at having saved a few *shekels*. The money is not the issue; the important thing is that he did not come out of there a *freier*. No-one has got the better of him. His dignity has been maintained. (The shopkeeper is no *freier* either. At the outset he had upped the price.)

Suckers for Sentiment

Israelis have been likened to the native cactus fruit, the *sabra*, which is covered with thorns on the outside yet is sweet and mushy on the inside. Music carries this emotionalism a long way, with Israeli 'golden oldies' making grown men cry, and nostalgic films on television receiving top ratings.

The Israeli national anthem, '*HaTikva*', features none of the thunderbolts and cannons and 'Conquer all others!' sentiments that dominate other anthems, just the simple line, 'The Hope', which is supported not by a march or royal trumpets, but by a surprisingly soft musical tune. Israelis only have to hear the opening notes to start reaching for the tissues.

Nearest and Dearest

At the centre of every Israeli's existence stands the family. Children are expected to grow up respecting their parents, to live at home until conscription age, to become lawyers or doctors, to marry into a good family (it can't hurt if they're rich as well), to reside in immediate proximity to their greying elders and to produce grandchildren ASATWO (As Soon As The Wedding is Over).

A somewhat cruel joke asks what the difference is between a Rottweiler and a Jewish Mama. The answer is that the Rottweiler will let go of the child eventually. The Jewish mama nurtures her babes from the age of 0 to 80 and insists on being involved in every aspect of their lives. With the advent of mobile phones, things have gone even further, with mothers calling their 19-year-old soldier sons to ask them if they need anything warm to wear, how the commander is treating them or if it's OK to bring them a nice sandwich.

Friendship for an Israeli is the second strongest value.

For men this applies especially to life-long army friendships. Two Israelis can spend three years in the army together, not hear from each other for 40 years, then meet by accident on the street and embrace with tears in their eyes.

An Israeli male is quite capable of enjoying a lovemaking session twice – once when he is engaged in it, and a second time when he regales his friends with the details. Indeed, the pleasure of basking in their admiration may exceed the physical one.

Obsessions With Possessions

A great many Israelis subscribe to the view that 'What you are is what others think you have'. They will go to extremes in order to upgrade their car to the very latest model just because their next-door neighbour has done so. When the government noticed a growing number of citizens depriving their families of essentials in order to have the newest car, it changed the licence plate numbering system so as not to indicate the year of registration. The car symbolizes success to an Israeli, and there is absolutely nothing worse than someone being more successful than you, leaving you feeling a total *freier*.

When Israelis go out in groups, say to a restaurant or café, the Israeli male will usually produce his wallet, car keys and mobile phone, and lay them on the table. This action serves a distinct purpose: by displaying these things he is 'claiming his territory'. The items carry obvious symbolism: the wallet to show wealth, the car keys to show wheels, and the mobile to imply important friends and connections. Walk into a café in Israel, and you will see a mountain of wallets, keys and phones on every table. When the waiter arrives with the order, it takes a while for it all to be shoved aside to make room for the food.

17

Behaviour

Driven to Extremes

The Israeli behind the wheel has to be seen to be believed. He thinks special rules apply on the road and the rules are these:

1. The road is a war zone and prisoners are never taken.
2. To be overtaken is a sure sign of impotence.
3. Since all drivers are crazy, one must drive like a raving lunatic to frighten off all competitors.
4. 'Accidents will never happen to me' (also known as the 'I am touched by God' syndrome).

When confronted about the way he drives, the Israeli will defend himself by saying: "If you want to get anywhere in Israel, driving like a maniac is the only way to get there."

The really scary thing on the road is not the bloodbath but the penalties. Speeding tickets are quite steep these days.

Opinions

For every two Israelis there are at least three opinions. Israelis like having strong views about everything, and there's nothing better than voicing them. Anyone lacking opinions, or appearing hesitant while making his point, is considered weak of spirit. A true Israeli speaks with the self-assurance and vehemence of a prophet. When confronted with facts that contradict his theory entirely, he will retort: "Why, that's exactly what I've been saying! You, my friend, have not been listening."

Impatience

Israelis have a very short fuse. They erupt when anything upsets them. Impatience is the norm. If you want to put this to the test, try attempting to overtake someone on the highway, or sitting in somebody's seat at the theatre or jumping the queue at the doctor's surgery. All will inevitably yield an outburst of anger, slurs, car-honking and so on. During their very first Hebrew lesson, newly arrived immigrants to Israel learn the word *'Savlanut!'*, meaning 'Patience!', only to discover that in Israel this is mostly a theoretical expression.

Pretence

There is nothing more satisfying to an Israeli than to play the game of pretend in his search for admiration. Every Israeli you meet has, by his own repute, spent his army years in a top combat unit (when in fact he was a cook in a base situated 100 metres from home). Israelis will say they run an "intimate boutique" (underwear store), "manage a transportation business" (drive a taxi) or "own a new executive automobile" (a 1979 Volvo, recently acquired, hence 'new' to the owner).

An Israeli listener never accepts such proclamations at face value. His trained ear automatically translates them into the truth.

Manners

In the everyday battle of survival in Israel, manners are usually, and casually, cast aside. Good manners are certainly taught at home by the family elders, but as the youngsters look about them whilst maturing, they reach their own very different conclusions about how to get things done, and uttering time-consuming niceties to strangers or standing for hours in queues is not included in the list. It has to do with their character of course. People with an exceptionally short fuse may start out standing politely in line but very soon become impatient. A common Israeli method of cutting in on queues in banks and other places is to work one's way to the front of the queue while declaring: "Excuse me, I only want to ask a quick question..." It is a ruse that always irritates all the others, who admonish themselves for not being the one doing the cutting in.

An Israeli is never coy about anything. Initiating a conversation with a total stranger on the bus, for instance, he may be overheard asking "Where do you work? How much money are you making? Really?! So why are you still working in that sweatshop?"

People also tend to stare at anybody who arouses their curiosity. It is not considered rude. In fact, it would be considered snooty not to stare at someone all your friends are staring at.

When they do encounter good manners, Israelis are taken by surprise. Kindness from an official, a man standing up when a woman enters a room, any sign of good and comprehensive service, and they are likely to say: "Why, this is like Europe. This is America!" A common misconception is to regard all Europeans and Americans as being invariably polite, while their own lack of courtesy is merely fodder for jokes, e.g:

An American, a Russian and an Israeli were contemplating the sign on a closed store window which said: 'Sorry, but we have a shortage of meat products.' "What does it mean – 'shortage'?" asked the American. "What does it mean – 'meat'?" mumbled the Russian. "Well I get it," smiled the Israeli, "but I have to admit, the first word has me stumped..."

Survivalists never see much point in politeness. Those who yield in a gentlemanly way to a rival in an argument are not considered polite but utter *freiers*.

20

Formal Is Not Normal

In Israel, formality is as rare as a month of unrelenting rain in the dead of winter. Children from kindergarten to university address teachers by their first names. Soldiers do this to their commanding officers and workers to their bosses. Nicknames are so common they are often used in preference to first names: an Israeli will address his boss by a nickname probably invented years before by neighbourhood kids, and no-one will think anything of it.

Formal wear is non-existent. Big and established companies have no dress code ('just don't come naked' is the general rule at work). At weddings the only one in a suit and tie will be the groom (who will struggle out of his costume as soon as the ceremony is over). An open-necked summer shirt, shorts and sandals is the real thing. Most Israelis never learn how to put on a tie. It's a foreign concept. The German organisers of a technology exhibition in Hanover took the time to distribute written instructions on 'How to tie a tie' amongst the Israeli businessmen roaming the halls.

Obsessions

News Addicts

Every hour on the hour, Israelis tune in to the radio news. Every half hour, they listen to the News Flash. Every day at 5 o'clock various TV channels lure viewers to watch their early evening news. A large section of the evening is devoted to watching at least two news programmes. Being up-to-date is of the utmost importance to an Israeli. News programmes start out with the political situation and security issues, next go over to business news, move on to world news reports, give special sports reviews and finish with a short lightweight piece and the weather forecast. Israelis often complain: "Every day the news is the same", or "The reports are always so horrible, I feel much better when I stop listening to the news", yet come evening they cannot resist turning on the television and absorbing news reports intravenously.

Mobile Manics

Israelis used to be a tad more relaxed individuals. That was when they had no mobile phones ringing. Nowadays it is not unusual to see a group of friends sitting around a table in a café, all engaged in conversation, each one speaking into his own phone, paying no heed to his table mates. Experts relate this behaviour to the Israelis' need to keep abreast of everything that is going on. Some say talking incessantly relieves tension (and who needs this more than the average Israeli?), while others maintain that it's an absolute necessity for everyone always to be together with their friends; if not in person, then at least in voice.

Custom and Tradition

Respect for the Sabbath

The word Sabbath (or in Hebrew, *Shabat*) is derived from the verb meaning 'to cease all physical work', which is precisely what is expected from every hard-working Israeli after a full week of earning one's bread. Its meaning contrasts starkly with the fact that most secular Israelis spend their Sabbaths slaving away at household chores or hiking with the kids and the in-laws, all of which might be considered to be hard work.

Sabbath falls on the Christian Saturday, thus Sunday,

for Jews, is the first working day of the week. In religious sectors of the community, the Sabbath is painstakingly guarded: from Friday evening until Saturday evening all traffic stops and people may be seen walking to Synagogue dressed in immaculate Sabbath clothes. It is forbidden for Orthodox Jews to answer the phone, to light a fire or cook, to switch electric lights on or off, or to do anything which might be considered work or might cause another Jewish person to work during the Holy Day.

In order to avoid people breaking the Sabbath laws, lifts go up and down day and night stopping at every floor so no-one has to press any buttons; computers turn the lights on in the house when the Sabbath starts and off once it is past; automatic heating-plates take care of the dishes prepared on Friday afternoon that are left to simmer. Lately, voice-activated devices have been introduced to help avoid all manual actions whatsoever.

Secular Israelis, however, take particular pleasure in proving they can act quite differently. Some secular shops are open on the Sabbath. People drive their cars everywhere, and on Friday nights clubs and cinemas are open. Yet even in the secular regions buses do not operate, all state facilities are shut and all banks and offices are strictly 'Shabbatting'. Naturally, friction occasionally occurs in areas where Orthodox and secular Jews attempt to co-exist. Some conflicts may even result in violence – a car straying into the empty streets of an Orthodox neighbourhood on the Sabbath might have stones thrown at it. Thus respect for the Sabbath is at times enforced, even if the method is somewhat unorthodox.

It Must Be Kosher

The word *kosher* is Yiddish for the Hebrew *kasher* which means, literally, 'good and true'. The laws of kosher food were prescribed in the Old Testament and were further developed in the Diaspora. Kosher laws come in abundance. Israelis who practise kosher eating daily know most of them by heart (but none of the grounds for their existence).

The main laws are as follows. It is permitted to eat animals that chew the cud and have cloven hooves (thus cow is permitted, but not pig or rabbit). It is permitted to eat birds (e.g. chicken), and it is permitted to eat fish but only ones with scales and fins (so, no eel, no catfish, no crabs, lobster, shrimp etc.). It is not permitted to consume meat and dairy products together (so no cheeseburgers – although some say that whatever constitutes a cheeseburger resembles nothing like real meat, and therefore they should be allowed).

The many laws of kosher eating are an example of how the Jewish faith is an intrinsic part of the everyday lives of Israelis. This is not to say all Israelis follow all the rules of Judaism to the letter. If you take a horizontal scale of faith, starting at one end with atheists and sliding along the religious path to the other end occupied by strict Orthodox Jews, most Israelis fall somewhere in the middle. Some will go to Synagogue to pray on holidays, yet drive on the Sabbath. Others will eat kosher foods only (complete with avoiding the consumption of meat and dairy products simultaneously), yet munch away on the Holy Day of Atonement which is strictly forbidden.

When asked "Are you religious?", many will answer "Yes, but I'm only 'a traditional'", meaning they allow themselves to embrace some traditions and decline others. This may appear inconsistent, but reasons for faith, any faith for that matter, are much more subtle than mere cold logic.

At any rate, it's better to have at least some fun in this life so that if there's no afterlife you won't have been a complete *freier*.

24

Two Laws in One Land

In Israel there is no separation between religious law and secular law. This fusion is encountered in the Israeli Declaration of Independence, which opens with the sentence: 'In the land of Israel, there rose the Jewish people...', and distinguishes Israel from other nations – a state rising out of religious circumstance.

There are two separate courts in Israel – orthodox and secular – each conducting its affairs independently, but the Israeli citizen must follow the rulings of both courts. This means that in many aspects of life, religion steps in. The laws of circumcision, marriage, divorce, burial and so forth are strictly religious and their origins can be found deep within Jewish history. For example, a law originating in the Old Testament obliges a wife seeking divorce to be granted a document of break from her husband (called a *get*), without which she must remain chained to him. Secular Israelis find it difficult to see the relevance of these laws in the modern age.

Even today any man whose last name is Cohen cannot marry a divorcee. The name Cohen means a priest, considered to be descended from the ancient priests of the Temple in Jerusalem. A Cohen is permitted to wed solely a maiden, an unmarried woman, one who is surely, as tradition holds, a virgin (tradition may so hold, but everyday life in modern Israel will mostly prove the opposite). This rule is related to faith in the future rising of the Third Temple: when the Messiah arrives, the Third Temple shall rise and all those who carry the Cohen name shall return to active priesthood. If, until that joyful moment, all Cohens insist on marrying only maidens, then they and their descendants will remain pure. If they marry divorcees, they will have tarnished this religious purity.

To be able to wed a divorcee, Mr Cohen and his beloved must travel outside the boundaries of Israel and marry in a secular ceremony conducted by a magistrate.

One of the most popular marriage sites is the island of Cyprus, allowing the couple a quick, sunny honeymoon after the ceremony before they fly back to Israel. Although this kind of marriage is unacceptable to the religious court, and these couples are considered married only by the secular state of Israel and not by the orthodox state of Israel, 'Cyprus Marriage Tour Packages' are promoted throughout the land by travel agencies and are filled with 'former priests' and their divorcee intendeds.

Susceptible to Superstition

Superstitions flourish in Israel. Some are common to other cultures: a black cat crosses your path while you're out strolling? Spit three times. Talking about future prospects? Knock on wood. Others are Israeli: bless your house with the 'House Blessing' – a wall plaque displaying phrases of blessing ('Let there be no curse in this house and let no pestilence come through this door…'); bless your car with a tiny 'Travel Blessing' card dangling from the rear-view mirror. The jet age produced a 'Flight Blessing', and for the computer age someone has invented a hilarious 'Internet Blessing' ('Let there be no virus in this hard disk and no malfunction in this keyboard…').

The ornament that hangs in most houses is in the shape of a hand with a blue eye fixed in the middle. This is the 'Hamsa', from north Africa that is believed to protect the house, its inhabitants and surroundings from evil. Many Israelis will deny being superstitious, yet if they were asked to empty their pockets, you are likely to discover a small Hamsa there, or a diminutive Book of Psalms, kept purely as protection from the dreaded Evil Eye.

Clairvoyants abound, and people spend time and money on crystal-ballers, palmists, and fortune tellers reading from coffee mugs, or even from surveying your buttocks. When someone breaks something expensive, showing the Evil Eye has been at work, it is customary to announce: "It's for atonement", and smile meekly. If you break a plate or glass in an Israeli restaurant, everybody automatically calls out cheerfully *"Mazel tov!"* ("Good Fortune!"), and beams at you, glad not to be the person who will have 'One broken plate' added to the bill.

Dates Apart

Israel uses two separate calendars simultaneously: the Jewish calendar (called in Israel 'the Hebrew Calendar') and the Christian calendar ('the General Calendar').

Israeli newspapers carry two different calendar dates. All holidays come and go according to the Hebrew calendar. Yet business in secular areas is conducted according to the General Calendar. It is a source of great confusion amongst Israelis themselves. Secular Israelis tend to forget all the relevant Hebrew dates, while religious Israelis make a point of bringing them up whenever they can – if only to spite their secular brothers.

Sense of Humour

At the funeral of the famous Jewish millionaire Baron Rothschild, one man tears his clothes with woe, falls to the ground in anguish and with a cry of desperation digs his fists into the dirt. One of the bereaved lends him a shoulder and helps him up. "Are you a close family member?" he asks with loving understanding in his eyes. "No," sobs the other, "That's why I'm crying."

Everyone knows the kind of Jewish humour which developed in the Diaspora as portrayed in such movies as *Fiddler on the Roof* – the kind of woebegone, we-are-toblame, self-mockery which sociologists now believe served as a form of psychological defence mechanism. When the nation settled, Jewish humour did not vanish. Since there is no-one like a *Paritz* (Polish landlord) to make fun of any more, most Israeli humour revolves around two subjects: politics and ethnic origin. What better way is there for eternal critics to complain than through humour?

Everyone is Ethnic

All stand-up comedy, if not political, deals with the way Israeli society is structured as well as with ethnic origins (accents, behaviour, etc.). To understand it, one needs to know that Israeli society divides into the following groups:

1. 'Ashkenazim' (European Jews), also known as 'Tzfonim' (Northerners). An alternative name is 'WuzWuzim' because East European Jews upon immigrating to Israel in the 1920s were unable to understand their surroundings and were frequently heard asking: "Wus?! Wus?!", which is Yiddish for "What?! What?!"

2. 'Mizrakhim' (North African Jews), or 'Dromim' (Southerners), otherwise known as 'TshachTshachim' (a mockery of the North African accent).

Then there are the more complicated smaller groups:

a. 'Arsim' – the Mizrakhim who live on the south side of the Tel Aviv area. They are dark skinned and are known to wear gold ornaments on their necks and arms.

b. 'Chnoonim' – who are Ashkenazim. They are pimple faced and pale skinned, wear round glasses and are versed in literature and mathematical algorithms (and known worldwide as nerds). Arsim dislike them intensely, and are therefore dreaded by every Chnoon around.

c. 'Yapim' – the northern Ashkenazim. They bleach their hair and have the obligatory single earring and a tattoo on their backs. They wear foreign designer fashion and listen to club music while surveying the world through sunglasses from which they are never parted (they even walk into night clubs under a full moon with their sunglasses perched on their heads).

d. 'Hippim' – the long-haired youths who have never quite accepted that the Sixties are long gone.

e. 'Rockerim' – long-haired youths who can't hear because they listen to heavy-metal music all the time at full blast. They wear dark clothes and believe the world will end within the next hour.

f. 'Dosim' – the Religious Jews. Secular Jews have a great time making fun of them since the two are so different yet to their sorrow or delight have to co-exist.

The Israeli stand-up comedian has all this from which to derive daily situations and funny characters. Israelis sit in the audience and roar with laughter, amazed at the society in which they live.

The Israeli Joke

Israelis are avid tellers of jokes. The Israeli joke is usually very long, and features characters, a plot and a moral behind the punch-line. People are not keen on one-liners; they feel it takes more skill to tell a story. A good joke teller is the Israeli equivalent of the European mediæval storyteller. No friendly lunch, night out on the town or beach-fire gathering would be complete without a joke or story being told.

To the Israeli joker, nothing is sacred. First and foremost he laughs about Israelis, and their incapacity to ever be satisfied:

In a plane full of rookie paratroopers, circling at 10,000 feet, the group is about to experience their first jump. The drill sergeant turns to the paratroopers and shouts above the engine's noise: "Now listen up! On my signal you jump! Your 'chute will open automatically after ten seconds. If it doesn't, pull on the reserve parachute. After you land a truck will be waiting to take you back to base. Any questions?…Good. Now – Go!"

The first soldier jumps. Falling through the air he counts out the ten seconds, yet his parachute fails to open. He tugs at the reserve chute – nothing. "That stupid sergeant!" he shouts as he plummets to earth, "He doesn't know what he's talking about! I bet there won't be a truck waiting when I land."

Holy matrimony is habitually ridiculed, as in the story about the husband who comes to the rabbi seeking advice: "I think my wife is trying to kill me," he says, "I believe she puts poison in my coffee." The rabbi proceeds to have a long talk to the wife before returning to the husband. "What should I do, rabbi?" asks the latter. "Drink the poison," rules the rabbi laconically.

Israeli systems come under constant ridicule, such as the education system in the following example:

The Regional School Inspector pays an unexpected visit to one of the local elementary schools. He walks into the classroom and faces the children. "Can you tell me who broke the two tablets with the ten commandments?" Silence. Suddenly one of the boys bursts out crying: "It wasn't me Inspector! I swear! I never broke any tablets in my life!" The Inspector turns to the teacher: "Who is this boy? Why doesn't he know the answer?" to which the teacher replies: "I know this boy, sir. Believe me, if he says he didn't do it, he didn't do it." Appalled, the inspector goes straight to the headmaster. "Outrage!" he shouts, "I ask who broke the two tablets and no-one knows! Not even the Bible teacher!" The headmaster looks at the Inspector briefly before pulling out his wallet. "No need to get upset, Inspector," he says, "how much can two tablets cost these days anyway? Now, to whom shall I write the cheque?"

Israelis will make fun of death, destitution and even religion and anti-Semitism:

Outside a church two Israelis read with interest a sign hanging on the door: 'Today Only! Become a Christian and receive $200 on the spot.' After a long deliberation they decide one of them will go inside, pretend to believe in Christ, and see what happens. The willing one steps into the dark interior and re-emerges half an hour later. "So? How was it?" asks his comrade. "Well, it was kind of fun. They sprinkled some water on me and read something in Latin and then asked me to repeat some other thing... and that was it" concludes the first. His friend can contain himself no longer: "And the $200? Did you get the $200?" "You Jews!" is the scornful answer. "It's all about money with you, isn't it?"

Government and Bureaucracy

Everything in Israel is either political or can be traced to politics. The reason Israelis take such an intense interest in government is that firstly, many decisions of government are security orientated and thus have a direct impact on the individual, and secondly, since the country is so young and is still in the making, for many people it is all a drama which is daily unfolding – so politics, though sometimes almost too disagreeable to behold, are essentially what will determine the next act in this extraordinary play.

Red Tape Versus Talent

In Israel, from the beginning, the public had to endure an excess of red tape. Everything was run by the State – hospitals, telecommunications, the airline, television, banks, plants, factories. An immigrant to Israel from the former USSR once stood for four hours in a queue at the bank, two more hours at the Social Security Office and three additional hours in a queue for paying bills at the City Hall. At the end of this he smiled at the bored official behind the opaque glass and remarked: "I come from Russia. You Israelis learn well. But we still do it better."

Living proof of socialism in action was the *kibbutz* concept. But with every *kibbutz* member wanting, and eventually getting, his own house and car and bank account, the socialism of the *kibbutz* died faster than its spiritual mentor, Soviet Russia. To the Russians, Israel never was as socialist as it could (or should) be. Khrushchev, visiting Israel in 1959, was quoted as saying: 'The microscope that could discover socialism in Israel is yet to be invented.'

He had a point. During its socialist heyday, the government wished to halt the purchase of colour televisions believing that this increased 'the socio-economic differences within Israeli society' because it encouraged people with no actual means to spend their last savings on such luxuries. It therefore scrambled the colour transmission of the then sole public Israeli TV channel. To the horror of viewers, episodes of *Dallas* instantly turned black and white. Press and public protested – to no avail. Then an Israeli engineer invented an 'un-eraser' (a reverse-scrambling device) which restored the colour when attached to the back of the TV set. In no time at all, the market became flooded with 'challenge the government' gadgets. Within a year, the government had grudgingly decided to cease the scrambling. Thus pure socialism got hammered by good old entrepreneurial talent.

Parliament and Party Games

The Israeli parliament is called the knesset (i.e. 'assembly'), a name held by the legislative presiding in Judaea in the 5th century B.C.

Until recently, the electorate cast one vote for their favourite party and another for their choice of Prime Minister. However, to everyone's discontent, this has been reduced to the party vote only. Should anyone wish to make a point of not wanting any of the candidates (a common and reasonable view), it is possible to cast a blank vote, which is separately counted and made into a statistic. More than 85% of Israelis turn out to vote. They all want their opinion to count; if they had three votes they'd use them all.

Israel is a model democracy, or at least aspires to be. The Knesset in Jerusalem contains 120 members and holds elections every four years, or earlier if things get messy. Every sector of the people can have its say, indeed there are so many small parties, with everything from Rights of Retired Citizens to Green Leaf (a party promoting marihuana use), that every decision always seems to be pending the resolution of party rivalries.

There is a Coalition and an Opposition, thus even the smallest of parties can put a vice around the Prime Minister with demands, or else cause the coalition to disintegrate. There are right-wing parties and left-wing parties. It used to be simple when the left was considered pro-Socialist, pro-Arab and pacifist and the right was seen as capitalist, or 'liberal', and hawkish. But even then it never really was that simple. Nobody wants socialism these days and the peace process has pushed everyone to the centre. The lack of distinction between right and left finds party members renouncing their own party and converting to the other side at a rate of once a month.

The public can come and go freely in the House of the Knesset and watch with awe the leaders working at leading – and hear with even more awe an abundance of slurs, swear words, shouting, name calling and harsh accusations. It is most definitely the best show in town and has been televised live for some years. Whenever there's nothing else on, Israelis may turn to channel 33, the 'action channel'.

They might even turn to *HaChartzoofim* (a single word combination of 'faces' and 'faeces'), a kind of Israeli version of the British *Spitting Image*, and no less remorseless in its depictions of political figures. Politicians are also caused considerable discomfort by the piercing satire of stand-up comedians. Typical of sentiments expressed about 'our leaders' is the joke about a frustrated Israeli who stepped into the reception hall of a local mental institution and declared his intention of having himself committed. "Why?" asked the man in the white coat, to which the prospective patient replied: "In this country there's only one difference between inside the asylum and out – at least in here the management is sane."

A Constitutional Conundrum

The law in Israel resembles the motley of people and bits of history that Israelis themselves are: some laws arrived from distant countries along with Jewish immigrants, others remain from the period of Turkish rule which lasted some 400 years, and some are left over from the British period. Most of these laws are sound, but a lack of cohesion exists and at times a lack of reason.

Israel has no written constitution. Every few years a weak voice is raised in parliament in favour of a constitution but gets shouted down. Everyone agrees that a constitution is a fine concept, but all want it to conform to their own inclinations. A constitution would determine the overall character of the state, and in Israel endless different groups are constantly pulling to make the country adapt to their own character.

Fine ideas like drawing up a constitution rarely have an easy path in a country like Israel. Nobody wants to be the *freier* who will lay down his personal interests for the good of the cause.

Presidential Prestige

The Israeli presidency is a rather odd institution and, like the British royal family, is mainly of a symbolic nature. The Prime Minister, who heads the government, is the one holding the power, while the President, elected by the parliament, is meant to be a non-political figure. The President represents the state of Israel to the world, and deals with delegations, ceremonies, speeches and other fine, stately affairs. The only power vested in this office is the power to pardon prisoners and set them free. The presidency, therefore, should in theory be a heaven and a haven for an elderly politician: he no longer has to quarrel with everyone, he has tons of respect, he still enjoys first-class trips overseas and is welcomed at the tables of emperors. Overall, at the end of a long career he can have a ball. It is most definitely a politician's dream retirement plan.

But many have had a tendency to voice political opinions, and as everything in Israel is political, to do so is tantamount to breaking the rules. Presidents are regularly accused of bending to the left or the right when they shouldn't bend at all. Consequently few are remembered fondly after their term ends.

Even the very thought of being president may be quite tiresome to some. Albert Einstein was approached with an offer to be the first Israeli president, yet gallantly declined. He clearly knew better, and some might say his decision was but another example of his truly superior mind.

Leisure and Pleasure

Holidays Are Hard Work

The Jewish faith has an abundance of holidays, and nowhere is this more evident than in Israel. Even the most irreligious will take part in a number of the many holiday ceremonies, some of which are 'religious' (evolved out of biblical laws), while others are 'historical' (evolved out of past events). Most holidays revolve around a story and a celebration, which can generally be summed up like this: "They tried to destroy us. They failed. Let's eat!"

Israelis pass up no opportunity for a holiday. The famous Jewish song 'Hava Nagila' attests to this. (*'Hava Nagila, Hava Nagila, Hava Nagila – Ve Nismecha*!') Even more popular outside Israel, it translates into words of great wisdom: 'Let us be merry, let us be merry, let us be merry – and happy!' Foreigners who do business with Israelis dread September. The Jewish New Year falls during this month and a deluge of holidays hits the land. For a full month, the sum total of working days is about ten, and trying to conduct business either from within or without the country is virtually impossible. Israelis will say to anyone wanting to close a transaction during this time: "After the holidays please, my friend. Only after the holidays..."

Out in the streets, parents drag bored, out-of-school-for-the-holidays children to holiday musicals, and people push their way into queues in malls and markets in the never-ending rush to buy food, presents and other means of bliss. Hordes cram airport concourses to get away on vacation.

The many holidays provide an opportunity for Israelis to pack the family in the car and head out to where everybody else is heading, mainly recreational campsites with a beach. Upon arrival, the kids rush into the water unheeding of parents' cries for sun-screen lotion, women watch over small children in the shade, while men light up the mandatory *mangal* (barbecue). Soon the air is filled with the smell of grilled meat and the sound of music. After eating, parents rest while the young ones play. At night parents sleep and the young still play.

The population divides roughly into two groups – the group that likes to camp (and have a barbecue), and the group that likes to walk. Each group looks down on the other: one believes that walking is for car-less student types who didn't get enough of it in the army, while the other maintains there's nothing to be gained from the outdoors solely by consuming meat in it.

The Israeli barbecue is an essential feature not only on vacation but – in secular homes – on Sabbath days as well. Guests are invited to witness the charring of the meat. All sorts of foods are laid out and every morsel is consumed. Conversation revolves around politics, sport and local gossip. Come evening, the guests leave and the hosts clear up, wash up and finally crash exhausted on their beds, ready for another week of work.

Nowadays the holiday spirit embraces several international customs including the appearance of Santa Claus icons in December, a multitude of parties on New Year's Eve and flowers on Valentine's Day, although none of these have any significance for the Jewish faith. Orthodox Jews object to this introduction of foreign holidays, but in Israel any reason to celebrate is good enough.

Fans for a Tan

Israel lies on the Mediterranean coast. Summer is long and hot, and people flood to the many beaches. Here they feel obliged to follow one all-important principle – be brown or be nothing. Melanoma may creep up on the sunbather one day, but what is that compared with smouldering looks from members of the opposite sex, surveying your tanned skin? Physicians may grimly shake their heads, but in Israel brown is healthy and young, while white is the unattractive opposite.

Israeli lifeguards (definitely not Baywatch types) use loudspeakers to bawl at the bathers. "You there, in the blue swimsuit! Move to the right! Are you DEAF?! I said move to the right!" People play matkot which resembles racket ball but has no purpose other than to bat the little rubber ball from one person to the other, while making as loud a sound as possible. Special 'matkot-game' areas are designated to try to protect participants from the complaints.

Some beaches are reserved for the religious and have signs reading: 'Men allowed on Sundays, Tuesdays and Thursdays. Women on Mondays, Wednesdays and Friday mornings. Full dress please!' Adjoining such areas one can find ultra-secular beaches ruled by youths of both sexes clad in the minimum amount of fabric allowed by law.

Visitors Are Welcome

Israelis love to visit and to have visitors. They nurture a lively concept called the Open House policy. While acquaintances are expected to phone before showing up, family members, close friends and even neighbours are expected just to appear at the door, carrying flowers or even better chocolates. A short ceremony ensues, when the gifts are passed from guest to host, while the traditional "*Shalom*" greeting is uttered.

Israelis have a special hiding place inside a cupboard where gifts are kept unopened so that they can be given when visiting other friends. A gift of chocolates may do the rounds for so long that if it were to be opened, the contents would be found to be grey with age.

When Israelis say "Why don't you stop by?" they really mean it and will be insulted if you don't. Visiting, for them, is to live life to the full – in other words to eat, talk, laugh, argue and, best of all, to complain.

The Ball Is All

Well, there's football (soccer, that is) and there's basketball and virtually nothing else. Every once in a while an Israeli will put Israel on the Map in an international competition in judo, cycling or tennis, yet few concern themselves with these sports on a daily basis. It is football that will keep two Israelis arguing heatedly for hours.

The sad truth is that Israelis, on an international scale, are not that good at football. As individual players they can be brilliant and are therefore hired by innumerable European teams. But as a team something seems to be missing – proper management for one thing, and discipline. When Israel played France on home ground some years ago and actually won (surprising Israelis as well as everyone else), the French team coach went on television, stared into the camera with tired, sad eyes, and in a melancholy voice said, "We just got beaten by the worst team in Europe." (He wanted to say "in the world", but that would have been too harsh.)

Sex and Sensitivity

Israeli men are considered macho by women and by themselves, and are expected to behave accordingly. Israeli women are tough, and the kind of cold look they nurture for local boys who try too hard may surprise foreigners, quite apart from the fact that some are in uniform, fully armed.

But things are changing, and the country is slowly breaking away from traditional views. New Israeli Men have appeared, crying at the movies and sensitive to women's ways. The age of sexual engagement is dropping, and parental concern is rising. It is now common practice for young couples to live together before marriage, an unthinkable proposition for the older generation.

The formerly respectable Government Institute of

Censorship has itself been censored to non-existence. These days Israelis want to see it all.

Late Night Life

Visitors to the land are impressed with the night life. Young Israelis usually leave their homes between 10 and 11 p.m., and return any time between 3 and 6 a.m. at weekends, slightly earlier on weekdays. It is not unknown for a tourist on his first night out in Israel to emerge from his hotel at 7 in the evening only to find empty pubs and closed discos. When he finally starts back to his hotel at 11, utterly disappointed, he is astonished to find hordes cramming the streets.

Eating and Drinking

Survivalists that they are, Israelis grow up knowing never to leave food on their plate. The Jewish mother likes to pile food on the plate and stand back, watching to make sure that the children are putting their jaws to good use. Leaving food on your plate is considered an insult to hungry children of third-world countries and is loudly condemned by parents. Food must be respected, so sweets are strictly reserved for the end of the meal, as is anything else which might spoil a good boy's appetite.

The National Dish

One of the problems the young nation of Israel faced upon creation was – what should be the national dish? Centuries of Jewish world-wide Diaspora had yielded countless recipes, all of which could be attributed to other nations. When each group of immigrants that came to Israel brought with them their own foods, a cultural battle-of-the-dishes began, with some delicious gastronomic results.

For a while it seemed that the oh-so-Jewish *tchulent* might take the stage as the Israeli national dish. Adopted by Jews everywhere (North African as well as East European), it is an aromatic stew of meat and beans, ideal for leaving to simmer on Friday afternoon for eating on the Sabbath. But perhaps because it carried with its aroma a certain smell of distant Jewish Diaspora and hardship, *tchulent* yielded to the young and exuberant *falafel* which is a practical dish and suited the new practical style adopted by all Jews when living in Israel.

Falafel is an art. Though Arab in origin, no nation can claim absolute ownership of it. The Egyptians started mashing their local kidney beans, formed them into balls, added spices and then deep-fried them in hot oil. In the area which is now Israel, the local Arabs were doing the same with their local beans ('*humus*', i.e. chickpeas). The hot and aromatic *falafel* balls are inserted into an Arab-style bread pocket ('*pitta*'), together with *humus* paste, salads and spices. The result is tasty, filling, and light on the pocket. Israelis adopted it instantly. Who in his right mind wouldn't? Even in times of strife, it is munched eagerly on both sides of the border, forever leaving *humus* smears on satisfied faces. Many Israelis still have their *tchulent* on the Sabbath, and savour its taste, yet on weekdays it's *falafel* that wins every time.

The Israeli Salad

In Israel one should never make the mistake of ordering salad on a full stomach. The dish that arrives on the table resembles a magic mountain. Every vegetable imaginable is there: lettuce, carrot, sweet corn, red pepper, onion,

41

along with nuts, cheese, olives, eggs, mayonnaise, all adorned with parsley and covered with virgin olive oil. It is always accompanied by fresh bread and butter and sometimes a steaming baked potato. This is when a visitor usually utters: "What's this? I only wanted some green leaves..."

Munchies and Crunchies

In Israeli homes there is always an abundance of munchies, or as they are commonly referred to, 'visitors' rations'. No Israeli larder will ever be without fried sunflower seeds, almonds, dried fruit (bananas, figs and papayas), small salty bagels, pretzels, fresh dates, potato chips and more. When the door opens to reveal unexpected visitors, a table is spread with these delicious nibbles, complete with at least three types of juice, jugs of iced-water with lemon and mint leaves, and a bowl of fruit, whatever is in season – peaches, melon, watermelon, white grapes, red grapes, apricots. Once everything has been consumed the hosts will announce that dinner is served, and everybody round the table rejoices – they're really going to eat now.

When Israelis go abroad for long periods, they yearn for foods that are found exclusively in Israel: real *humus* paste and *techina* (ground sesame seeds with olive oil, parsley and salt); Café-Elite – an old-fashioned brand of instant coffee scorned by coffee snobs but loved by Israelis; *bamba* – a yellow munchy, made of peanut butter and corn, that they chew on from teething age; and the assortment of crunchies such as nuts and baked sunflower seeds which feature prominently in any Israeli's life.

Every Israeli has relatives living abroad, and whenever he announces he is about to honour them with his presence he will be flooded with requests for *bamba* and Café-Elite, real *techina* and bags of crunchies. In such circumstances it doesn't pay to be mean.

Drinking with Discretion

Until quite recently the ordinary Israeli was not used to drinking much. Wine was mainly used in religious ceremonies (the quality verged on cleaning fluid), and in the pubs and bars there was beer – usually local brews that made everybody's head spin. Even today an Israeli in a pub will sip at a single beer for hours, until it is the temperature of soup. The Israeli pub, or what Israelis call a 'restaurant-pub', is a combination of American bar with high stools and European dim-lit atmosphere.

However, as they began to travel and returned from their trips carrying French wine and Kentucky rye whiskey, they brought about a silent revolution. These days in most pubs one can find Australian lager sitting neck to neck with Belgian monastery brew.

Israeli taste itself is becoming more sophisticated. An Israeli might be heard casually remarking to the bartender: "Give me a White Russian, and easy on the ice. And by the way, I didn't care for the Rusty Nail you made the other night. You did make it with Scotch, didn't you?..."

Health and Hygiene

"The most important thing is health!" is an expression used even by those Israelis who smoke three packs of cigarettes a day, devour rump steak and ice cream for lunch and lie on deep-cushioned sofas flipping from one television sports programme to another for exercise.

The number one cause of death is heart and vascular disease. Number two is cancer. This is not surprising in a nation so stressed. But one of the greatest killers in Israel is neither smoking nor alcohol nor war nor terrorism, but car accidents. If anything could ever be characterised as a plague in Israel, it is the smashing of one vehicle into another, both driven by righteous drivers.

Women tend to live longer in Israel, for as every Israeli knows, "A Jewish wife is unwell, weak, sick, ailing, suffering, and finally a widow". The average woman lives to the age of 79. Men depart earlier on in the course of things (average 74), which stands to reason, seeing that most Israeli drivers are male.

A Bitter Pill to Swallow

A new national Health Insurance Plan requires citizens to pay a progressive insurance fee, deducted each month from their salary, towards health funds. This has affected their take-home pay, giving Israelis another reason for complaint, but no-one doubts that the level of treatment is on the rise and that everyone will benefit.

However, things are not that peachy. Doctors in Israel, even those at an extremely high professional level, are not paid very much in hospitals (most of which are still state owned), and consequently they practise in private clinics that keep setting new standards for the term 'expensive'. Those who work solely for the state hospitals are bitter and tired. Every few months a doctors' strike is announced, to the great discomfort of patients. When Israelis wake up to news of yet another strike they tell each other: "Have a good day and remember there's a strike on, so try not to be ill…"

It's All in the Wash

Israelis do not and will not, under any circumstances, keep the washing machine in the kitchen. For them it would be unhygienic to put dirty laundry and consumable food in dangerous proximity. Most people live in flats with no garden, so adjoining every Israeli bath- or shower-room is a small room dedicated to laundering. It has a little window which allows access to laundry lines. Some of the juiciest gossip is exchanged between neighbours while hanging wet clothes out to dry. When Israelis who grow up in flats build a house, they choose to install a laundry room over any other option.

Because of the heat, homes in Israel do not have wall-to-wall carpeting. Vacuum cleaners are reserved for rugs, sofas and car seats. The heat generates enough dust and dirt to create dust-balls the size of tumbleweeds, so the floor needs constant cleaning. For this Israelis use a Sponja – an enlarged version of the T-shaped device often used to clean car windscreens. The process of cleaning the floor with this implement involves a special rag and a lot of soapy water, and the delight of having your bare feet in cool water on a hot day is enough to urge you to clean the floor even when it's spotless. Sponja sticks are used nationwide. They never fail to satisfy.

Systems

The Tel Aviv Subway

The Tel Aviv Subway is a myth. Every visitor to the humming metropolis, suffocating in traffic and suffering from insufficient parking spaces, will agree: "This place needs a subway – and fast." The reason there isn't one is a mystery. A plan for a comprehensive Tel Aviv Subway has existed since 1958. It is whispered that British and French companies volunteered to carry out the work in return for royalties, yet were declined. Many politically motivated mayoral candidates promised to realize the prophecy of a functioning subway in return for a seat in City Hall, yet failed to live up to the task.

Meantime the years flew by. War came and then peace,

but the subway never materialized. Since Tel Aviv had grown rapidly, the original blueprints had ceased to be sufficient. Moreover, the government had, over time, relinquished ownership of most of the land in the city centre, so any attempt to construct the subway would involve compensating inhabitants for drilling tunnels beneath their homes.

When, in 1999, yet another Prime Minister and another mayor announced their intention to "lay the cornerstone of the first subway station in Tel Aviv" and proceeded to hold a big press conference and ceremony, it was hard to stop the laughter.

Israelis have changed the old saying: 'When the Messiah arrives, he shall come on a white donkey', to: 'When the Messiah arrives, he shall emerge, magnificent, out of the Tel Aviv Subway.'

Taxes Are Taxing

Income tax combines with VAT, purchase tax, health insurance tax, social security tax and customs to level about 50% taxation on the income of the average bread-winner. One Israeli, wanting to make a point, wrote to the Israeli Revenue Service suggesting that he be left with what he usually gave to the state and let the state take what he was usually left with.

The result is a culture of tax evasion. Employees have no choice but to pay up, but the self-employed (such as business owners) submit an annual income tax report to the IRS. The majority report considerably less than their actual income. In an attempt to curb tax evasion, the government published a book listing all self-employed people in Israel, along with their declared incomes. The book became a best-seller. Everybody roared with laughter as they read the pitiful income figures declared by some of the country's richest men.

From Drought to Deluge

Israelis may believe that two weeks of straight rain after seven months of dry heat is extreme (and by local standards it is), but compared with other parts of the world it is nothing more than a light shower. It is no wonder Israelis call the toilet flush 'the Niagara'.

The water system in Israel is perpetually on the brink of bankruptcy, not for lack of funds, but for lack of water. Bitter wars have been fought in the region since Abraham's days over the control of water sources. When the country is hit by drought, anyone caught cleaning his vehicle with a hose, instead of using an old bucket and rag, will be fined for wasting valuable water. This makes sense in a country which sometimes has to resort to buying drinking water from neighbouring Turkey in order to survive.

Many first-time visitors to Israel are astonished by the aridity of the land. (Hebrew has special names for the first rain and the last rain of the year.) Not even the Sea of Galilee would make it into the European lakes league. From childhood people the world over carry a vision of rushing water when they hear the words 'the River Jordan'. How could the magnitude of the Bible tales not depict a river so grand, a spectacle so impressive, as to make even the Rhine look like a creek? But in reality the Jordan is the equivalent of a European stream. It is a known fact that Joshua's words to the Israelites as they came to cross the Jordan en route to the Holy Land were: "And now – everyone please take a big step."

Israel does have a winter period – December to April, when temperatures drop and rain falls. But the rain seems to take everyone by surprise, as well as most of the systems. Street lights go out. Home heaters overwhelm the country's electrical supply. Roads are flooded, and the dust and oil which collect on the asphalt during the hot summer months turn the surfaces into greasy skid-pans.

When this happens Israelis will sit in their stationary cars, in the rain, in the traffic jam gradually engulfing the country, and curse silently.

When there is a really harsh winter (once every seven years or so), snow falls on the mountain tops and, most significantly and romantically, on Jerusalem. All systems in the capital come to a halt: buses, taxis, schools, offices, trains. Tel Avivians dive into their automobiles and hurry towards the Holy City to get a glimpse of the Dome of the Rock in its white veil. Moments later the ferocious Israeli sun breaks through the clouds and melts away the snow, along with all hope for an unplanned day off.

Educational Extras

One of the basic laws in Israel is the Bill of Free, Mandatory Education, though the 'free' gets a bit blurred as the government finds it difficult to stump up for textbooks, notebooks, pencils, rulers, school bags, school lunches and especially class trips, so parents can find themselves going to extremes of expense in order to have an educated offspring in the house. Israelis point out that, in Hebrew, the 'Bill of Free Mandatory Education' constitutes the apt abbreviation: 'Ha.Ha.Ha.Ha'.

Education in Israel consists of six years in elementary school, three in junior high and three in high school. After that comes military service.

Join the Army Then See the World

All Israelis are soldiers. Whether in uniform, carrying arms, or strolling down the street in civilian clothes, they are soldiers. Army life starts when children go on school trips accompanied by a soldier carrying a rifle. "Can I have one?", the children ask, pointing at the gun, at which the soldier laughs and promises, "When you grow up, you'll be sure to have one." Women serve for 18 months while men spend three years in uniform.

Once discharged from military duties, every Israeli boards the first aeroplane bound for either South-East Asia or South America. This started some years ago when Israelis, who felt they needed to get away from it all, actually went. The post-army trip can be summed up in one sentence – 'Travel as far and for as long as your money may take you', and it usually lasts between six months and a year. One result of this is that people in countries such as India are positive Israel must be an empire to produce such a multitude of travellers. Another is that entire streets in cities like Bangkok are plastered with signs in Hebrew. Israelis are fond of spreading Israeli culture, and it would not be odd to come upon an old man in a place such as Halong Bay, Vietnam, enthusiastically singing 'Uga-Uga' (an Israeli children's song) with a toothless grin.

Much of the slang and the euphemisms used in everyday language comes from army life. For example, "This is divided into three parts…" (everything in the army divides into three parts), or the army way of saying "Affirmative!" for 'Yes' and "Negative!" for 'No'. Two middle-aged secretaries might be overheard starting a dialogue thus:

"Miri, are you there?"

"Yes."

"Yes what?!"

"Yes Sir Sergeant!"

"That's better…"

Israeli men are required to do reserve army training for a period of one month every single year of their lives until the age of 45. Consequently Israelis say that an Israeli citizen is merely a soldier on 11 months' leave.

When the time comes, the reserve soldier puts on his uniform and reports to base. Some actually like this period, saying it is good to reunite with old army comrades, feel young again and distance oneself from everyday struggles. Most reserve army sessions are spent guarding distant army posts, reading the sports sections of newspapers and playing Israel's number one board game – backgammon. Tournaments may last for weeks.

A Testing Time

At the age of 21, after three years in the military when youths of other nations are emerging into the commercial world degree in hand, an Israeli male may just be thinking of going to university. He may already be married or about to be married and more concerned with finding a part-time job and keeping a roof over his head.

University is expensive. Israelis look longingly at such countries as Germany and the Netherlands where university education is made available to the masses. (Only in the US is it more expensive than in Israel.)

Israeli universities are world renowned – Tel Aviv for law, Jerusalem for medicine, the Ben Gurion in Beersheba and the Technion in Haifa for science – and attract many foreign students. The demand for places has overwhelmed supply in Israel, so before you may even apply for a place, you have to endure a lengthy psychometric test, the object of which appears to be simply to test your ability to pass psychometric tests.

A prerequisite for a university education is a high level of competence in English. Non-compliance will result in non-entrance, or having to study English while at university which nobody wants to do. Everyone thinks English lessons are supposed to end with high school, and American TV sitcoms will do the rest.

As hostels and residences are scarce and are offered almost exclusively to foreign students, most Israeli students have to find their own accommodation. Paying for everything means that everyone has to work, so there is a proliferation of jobs for students. Recollections of university years for most Israelis are therefore less of the "Those were the best years of my life, when I played games all day and chased blondes around the campus all night" type, and more "I was working like a mule and dying to get my degree – and leave".

Those who wish to study law must demonstrate higher than average grades and test results, a fact which leads to many applicants being turned down. Some board the first London-bound plane in order to enrol at an English law college. Israel permits the study of the basics of law in England, as long as the returning graduate undergoes a crash course in Israeli law, after which permission to practise law in Israel will be granted. Thus England acts as a refuge for Israeli youngsters who seek the bar. This is Israeli revenge for the years of British Mandate.

Culture

Years of immigration to Israel have produced a diverse culture. Immigrants used to keep to themselves, each group engrossed in its own cultural expressions, but the younger generations are beginning to mix them all together. Second-generation East Europeans produce music with Yemeni rhythm, while descendants of North-African Jews perform in plays written originally in Yiddish. Israeli culture is consequently hard to define. Its strongest characteristics are its diversity and richness. Two main streams are evident: one is adherence to Jewish themes, the other is the deep-rooted appeal of politics.

The Jewish nation has always referred to itself as The People of the Book (a name given to it by Mohammed), since it believed the Jews bequeathed to the world the Old Testament, written originally in Hebrew. The founders of Israel wanted a nation built upon solid ground of literature and thought. Things have got a bit out of hand, however, as TV mega-malls and Sega arcades have been built upon the wreckage of old bookstores. The world trend of on-screen entertainment has pushed the children of the Book towards the computer console.

Literature

Israel features a vibrant writers' scene, and some are prominent both in Israel and beyond. Amos Oz is one: his book *My Michael* (which describes the emotional tribulations of an Israeli couple following the Six Day War) is widely read and regularly studied in Israeli schools.

The stories of S.Y. Agnon, winner of the 1966 Nobel Prize, are written in classical Hebrew (with layer upon layer of different meanings). They depict the lives of Jews in Galicia, where folk stories, legends and mysticism live side by side with daily events in the Diaspora of the last century. Agnon is greatly respected by the state of Israel and is featured on the 50 *shekel* note.

For Israelis, art should be serious and profound. Art exists to make one ponder. If an art form is amusing, Israelis treat it purely as entertainment. The works of Ephraim Kishon are an exception. A master of humour, his poignant satires, depicting Israelis (be they politicians or ordinary folk) in various situations, are the embodiment of the Israeli spirit. One of his short stories describes an old door-to-door vendor of shoelaces and buttons from whom nobody ever buys anything. One day a householder has a sudden change of heart and asks for shoelaces. The old man says he has none. The householder then asks for buttons, at which the old man turns pale and has to reveal that the ancient box he carries is empty. Nobody, he explains, ever buys anything anyway, but one has to do something with one's life, doesn't one?

Poetry

Israel's national poet is Chaim Nachman Bialik. His poems depict Jewish secular/orthodox conflicts as well as inner feelings of longing for peace, homeland and happiness. They have become a symbol of the bridge Jews have crossed from the Diaspora to Israel, and from tradition to secularity. Quite a few have been put to music and are among the most beautiful Israeli songs – for example:

Cover me with your wings,
And be my mother, my sister.
And let your bosom be my sanctuary,
The nest of my forsaken prayers.

And at the time of mercy, the twilight time,
Lean towards me and I will confess the secret of my agony:
They say, there is youth in this world –
Where is my youth?...

Cinema

Israelis are good at making sentimental films depicting 'the little man', usually a hard-working next-door neighbour, and his tribulations in Israeli society. Such films never fail to receive international acclaim. *The Summer of Aviya,* starring actress Gila Almagor, is a touching tale of her childhood in which she plays her own mother. Another famous film, directed by Kishon, is *Salach Shabati*, the story of the harsh life an immigrant endures in Israel in the 1950s, living in bad conditions and trying to support his large family and keep his sanity, portrayed with humour and a touch of naïveté. It had such an impact in Israel it was turned into a successful musical, and is a story treasured by Israelis all their lives.

One performer who was a smash hit upon world stages with performances like *Fiddler on the Roof* is Chaim Topol. He is nothing short of inspirational to Israeli actors who know full well that, in order to succeed on world stages, one has first to lose the very distinct Israeli accent, and that this, in itself, is a talent.

Music

The Jews have always been drawn to music. Hundreds of thousands of immigrants from Europe and the former USSR brought violins with them in their suitcases, while immigrants from Africa and Asia could not be parted from the Ud (Arab plucking instrument) and drum.

The Israeli Philharmonic Orchestra is known world-wide, and names like Itzhak Perlman, Pinchas Zukerman and Daniel Barenboim are examples of Israeli musicians who have made it into virtuoso history.

Israeli contemporary music is not just popular in Israel. In London, for example, one may find CDs by Rita, Ofra Chaza or Achinoam Nini (under her stage name, Noa). These artists who combine European and Middle-Eastern elements in their music are true examples of the cultural melting pot of Israel.

Business
Quality and Qualifications

While in some countries formal qualifications are the only ticket to a paying job, in the Israeli job market experience counts, sometimes even more than formal qualifications. One who has proven experience in computer programming, for instance, will be hired faster than someone who has just emerged from university with a degree in computer engineering yet with no practical knowledge. For survivalists, it is having come through the jungle alive which counts, not the studying of the fauna and flora.

Nevertheless, the newly hired employee is expected to gain formal qualifications if he has none (and many people continue to study while working, hence the proliferation of academic institutions providing evening classes). If he does not, his chances of promotion to management are slim. Besides, the management might look like *freiers* if they embraced someone who had skipped getting his formal qualifications for why should they have suffered when this newcomer has not?

The typical candidate for promotion will be someone who was an officer during his army service. The fact that a typical army officer's skills include wasting this year's budget so as to ask for more the next year, following orders from above without question, and threatening subordinates into submission with prison sentences, does not at first seem to deter managers from accepting such a candidate into their ranks. After all, they themselves were all once army officers.

Men in Business

The best and worst of Israeli characteristics come together to create the Israeli businessman. As a survivalist, he will strive for the goal alone, improvising endlessly to achieve success. He will always emerge from any negotiation with a minimum of apparent victory (if not an actual one) due to his primal need to avoid being a *freier*. Negotiating is a skill that true Israelis are born with. "Haggle about everything, for life is a *shuk*!" (a market place), so always try to get it cheaper or sell it dearer.

The Israeli businessman will not stand for formalities (titles and surnames, small talk, long business dinners) and will try to cut to the chase whether or not his opponent is ready. He will complain endlessly and thus appear to his colleagues to be earnest and responsible. He will worry, and talk about business being "far too slow",

55

which carries that great plus: being pleasantly surprised when things actually go right.

Women in the Workplace

In a country where all men are literally eternal soldiers, there is a blatant lack of equality for women (though many male Israelis will strongly deny this). Inequality starts in kindergarten, where girls sing songs of brave men, and goes right through the education system where, due to the low level of pay, men prefer to leave teaching to the women. Fewer women than men study computer technology, mathematics and physics which later yield well-paid jobs. In the highly religious sectors of society, a woman's place is usually at home, raising children.

Although women comprise 35% of the workforce, the exceptionally low number of women in parliament shows the long way Israeli society has yet to go on the road to equality of the sexes. Israeli businesswomen (such as Pnina Rosenblum with her brilliant career in fashion and cosmetics) are so rare they have become a myth in their own lifetimes.

Office Politics

Though to an outsider who visits an Israeli company everything looks informal and friendly, strict rules of hierarchy control the offices (one has only to recall that Israelis have all been in the army where everybody is under somebody else). Some managers do not like to fraternise with their subordinates (referred to as "keeping the distance" – a phrase derived, naturally, from army life), while other bosses will share a joke or a laugh with everybody ("breaking the distance"). Informality can lead to uncertainty about who is friend and who is foe, so office politics flourish. Israelis are good at taking credit for success and blaming others for failures. The Israeli precept is: 'Failure is an orphan while success has many fathers'.

Industry and Innovation

Israelis have achieved world renown in a number of fields. The diamond industry is one. Today Israel serves as a world centre for diamonds, importing rough diamonds, cutting, polishing and then exporting them, to the degree that everywhere in the diamond business transactions are concluded with the Hebrew words: "*Mazel ubracha*" – "Good fortune and a blessing".

Other exports from Israel to destinations such as the USA, China, Japan and EU countries include machinery (mostly from the extensive Israeli military industry – anything from hand-guns to aeroplanes), chemicals (Israelis milk the Dead Sea for its minerals and chemicals to produce salt, bromine, phosphates, therapeutic mud and even perfumes), textiles (swimsuits – what else in a country as hot?), and agricultural machinery and produce.

The nation's agriculture is held up as an example of what people can achieve in a country poor in natural resources. Its citrus fruits, grapes, watermelons, tomatoes are presented in markets worldwide, and Dutch flower dealers are more than familiar with Israeli flowers (which account for one quarter of agricultural exports from Israel). Yet one third of the land is barren desert and most winters yield not one month of proper rainfall.

The Israelis' patented legacy to the agricultural world is the drip irrigation pipeline. Instead of spraying water all over a field, long plastic pipelines criss-cross the field, each with special patented valves placed along it which release a drop of water at a time to feed the plant sited next to it. The result is not only water saved but extremely effective weed control.

Another first, produced for the medical market, is a camera the size of a vitamin pill, which is swallowed so that it can send back voyager images of the intestines.

Crime and Punishment

In the presence of foreigners, Israelis will show great pride in the relatively low rate of crime in their country. Between themselves, however, they will confess to being truly concerned with Israel's fast-growing similarity to other parts of the Western world. Yet violent crime is statistically rare, even in the big cities. Walking at night alone (if you're male) or in groups (if you're female), is still considered safe in any part of Haifa or Eilat.

The relatively low crime rate is generally attributed to the fact that Israelis do not drink much, and it is very uncommon to see displays of public drunkenness. Society being fairly traditional certainly helps, and army life uses up a lot of youthful energy which might otherwise be channelled elsewhere.

The exception to the low crime-rate statistics is car theft, as the amazingly high rates of car insurance attest. Behind the unpleasant experience of discovering one bright morning that one of your most prized possessions has vanished during the night stands what appears to be an entire industry of thieves who trade with used parts dealers (who 'don't want to know' where the parts came from), who in turn deal with dodgy body shops (who never ask questions), who are in business with insurance companies (who are, naturally, above reproach), and the chain continues.

Since the tax on a new car is almost 100%, even the state could be said to have a vested interest.

Most thieves come from and disappear into the Palestinian Territory, so the Israeli police are powerless to control the thefts. When, some years ago, the Palestinian rulers eloquently declared that any car stolen in Israel would become registered by law in their own territory, the absurd reached hitherto unheard-of levels.

Foul Fines

It is said that there are three generations of Israelis: the ones who built the country, the ones who took it all for granted and littered it, and the ones who now have to clean up the mess. Today, if an Israeli wishes, he can become a 'cleanliness trustee' on behalf of the city council, and by law has the right to fine anyone he may spot dropping litter within the city boundaries.

The crime of littering is not limited solely to members of the human race. In most cities the fouling of the pavement by a dog will result in a heavy penalty for the creature tied to the other end of its leash.

Conversation

Bad Words and Gestures

For Israelis, there are 'bad' words and there are 'really bad' words. The bad words are in Hebrew and were invented inside army tents or on the street. The really bad words in general come from Arabic. Israelis maintain that to curse in Arabic is just 'juicier'.

Phrases beginning with '*Ina-al...*' are bad, while words said in a furious whisper containing such sounds as continuous 'ssssss' or 'xxxxxx' are very, very bad.

The Yiddish word "*Nu*" when said impatiently means "Come on then, get on with it!" This is commonly answered by the phrase: "*Lama ma kara?*" (meaning: "What the hell's going on?", but short for "What on earth has happened for you to make such a fuss?"). The latter is accompanied by an aggressive twist of the palm of the hand towards the face of the person to whom the gesture is directed. "*Lama mi ata?!*" is a common variation and means "Who do you think you are?!" Most of these expressions are said in jest, and are daily figures of speech.

When others are talking, Israelis find it difficult to control their impatience and constantly interrupt with "of course, of course", or "yes, yes!", to show that they got the point long ago so there is no need for you to go on. They gesture while talking, and in the midst of a heated argument flailing arms may even hit innocent bystanders.

As Israelis delight in cellular conversations, mostly using an almost invisible earpiece, they can be spotted in the streets (or even floating on their backs in the Dead Sea), talking and gesticulating apparently to no-one in particular. The very first Israelis to do this were openly regarded as insane. Nowadays everyone is equally bonkers.

Conversational Taboos

There are three fundamental issues in Israel which Israelis constantly contemplate, discuss and argue about: security (what foreign news refers to as 'The situation in the Middle East'), religion (Jews vs. Christians vs. Moslems vs. …), and naturally, The Holocaust.

Since opinions amongst Israelis abound, debates can be volatile. Foreigners who converse with Israelis on these topics are at a disadvantage from the start. Israelis consider non-Israelis to be little more than babes about these issues. They believe that personal involvement increases one's capacity for understanding, and therefore only Israelis can fathom the intricacies. If an outsider expresses views on these subjects, he is inadvertently breaking a taboo. If he proves knowledgeable, most Israelis are truly amazed. They might even let him finish without interruption.

Language

The resurrection of the 2,000-year-old Hebrew language into the living world of modern Israel is a story unparalleled in human history. For a thousand years Hebrew remained a holy language to be used on special occasions only – in religious ceremonies and as a means for Jews from different parts of the globe to communicate with one another, since Jews spoke a hundred different languages. It was called The Tongue and hardly developed at all until the late Middle Ages, when poets dared to use it for writing poetry. From that time on, with every small Jewish push towards the return to Israel and a farewell to the Diaspora, Hebrew became increasingly used on secular occasions.

Some Jewish leaders were far from comfortable with the idea of daily, secular Hebrew, but a century ago a man called Eliezer Ben Yehuda gave it a final push when, against all odds, he chose to educate his children exclusively in Hebrew. In the midst of the 20th century an argument raged amongst Jewish leaders as to whether the official language in Israeli schools should, in fact, be German. The battle ended with Hebrew prevailing.

Modern Hebrew is constantly evolving. As a language that has not been in everyday use for very long, it lacks words to describe modern things. The official business of the Academy of the Hebrew Language is to invent new Hebrew words. Anyone can send in suggestions for new words, and if accepted, they go into the lexicon. Whether or not the man in the street accepts these inventions is a totally different matter. More often than not the new word 'dropped' into the mouths of the citizens seems too ludicrous to use and remains a theoretically correct word, to dwell forever unused inside the Hebrew Dictionary. (For example, the correct Hebrew word for telephone is *sachrachok* which means 'speak afar'. No Israeli ever uses this word, except of course when playing Scrabble.)

Hebrew is the original language of the Bible which in the English version contains many pure Hebrew words. How many English-speaking people know the true meaning of such biblical words as Bethlehem, Nazareth, Benjamin, Moses, or the original name of Christ – Jeshua?*

Hebrew features in the background of most of Western history. During the Middle Ages, for example, schools of medicine from Leipzig to Padua were frequented by many Jewish students, and many lessons were conducted in Hebrew. The Puritans, arriving in America in 1620, believed Hebrew to be the word of God because the Bible was originally written in Hebrew, and they studied it to the degree of fluent speech. Their descendants were responsible for establishing such colleges and universities as Harvard and Yale (the emblem of Yale, to this day, displays Hebrew words), and taught Hebrew as part of the very first curriculum of these institutions.

Spoken Hebrew today is constantly being influenced by other languages, firstly by English, for in the new technological world English reigns supreme, and secondly by Arabic, a sister language to Hebrew (yet not at all the same). Arabic's influence is mainly in slang. It is officially the second language of the State of Israel, but this doesn't mean all Israelis can speak both languages. With politics involved, almost all Arab citizens know Hebrew, but few Jewish citizens know any Arabic to speak of, or in.

Yiddish

Two streams of special Jewish languages evolved in the Diaspora: Ladino and Yiddish. In the Balkan countries and Northern Africa, where Jews went after being exiled

*Respectively, House of Bread, Guardian, Son of my Right Hand, Pulling out of the Water, and Salvation.

from Spain in 1492, a mixture of Hebrew and Spanish developed. This language was called Ladino. In the Israel of today it is a dying language, spoken by a few elderly people.

In Europe through the Diaspora years a mixture of Hebrew, German, Slav and a few other languages formed Yiddish – the word meaning simply Jewish. Yiddish is declining: the elderly still enjoy theatre, newspapers and books in Yiddish, but their grandchildren will only study Yiddish at university, much like people may study Latin in Europe.

The Jewish legacy to other languages mainly consists of phrases from the Yiddish. In America, and especially in New York where many Jewish immigrants settled, a number of Yiddish words colour the English language: *schmaltz* – oily sentiment, *mensh* – an honourable person, *kvetch* – whine, *schlep* – drag or carry, *klutz* – a dolt, *schmooze* – chat up, *nosh* – snack, *shtik* – piece, *nudnik* – a pest, *glitch* – slip or slide, *shlemiel* – an unlucky person, *kibosh* – prevent, *spiel* – story, *putz* – a fool, *shtum* – quiet, *pisher* – a squirt, *schnozzle* – nose, and the cry of woe *Oi vay!* are words that Jewish and non-Jewish New Yorkers use regularly. These are all considered quite *kosher* for daily use.

Yiddish is an extremely rich language, full of humour, taste and colour. It is a common belief that some jokes can only be told in Yiddish, and once translated into other languages, lose their edge. For example, the Yiddish word *shoin* means 'never mind', and must be accompanied with arms making a dismissive gesture. A story describes a stuttering Jew who, seeing his wife Shoshana walking unawares towards an open pit, cries out in horror: "Sho..! Sho...! Sho...! ...Shoin".

The Author

Born in Israel, Aviv Ben Zeev attributes his Angst to a father of German descent and his temper to a mother who came from Argentina, a combination that made him a bit eccentric. Growing up he learned to take nothing for granted and to try never to be a *freier*.

After four years in uniform that looked particularly bad on him, he waved aside what could have been a brilliant career as a second-rate classical guitarist, and set out on his post-army trip. In the course of this he found himself in a college in New Zealand, teaching about Israel, and at the University of the Kingdom of Tonga, amusing students with tales from the Holy Land. He also discovered a passion for airports.

Having joined the circle of telecommunication company employees, it is in airports that he may be found most of the time, en route to this or that remote country. His home, all too infrequently inhabited, is situated in the bustling heart of Tel Aviv where he can sometimes be spotted circling about in his car, searching in vain for a parking space. All in all trying to keep his place – on the Map.